Nature's Children

TIGERS

Bill Ivy

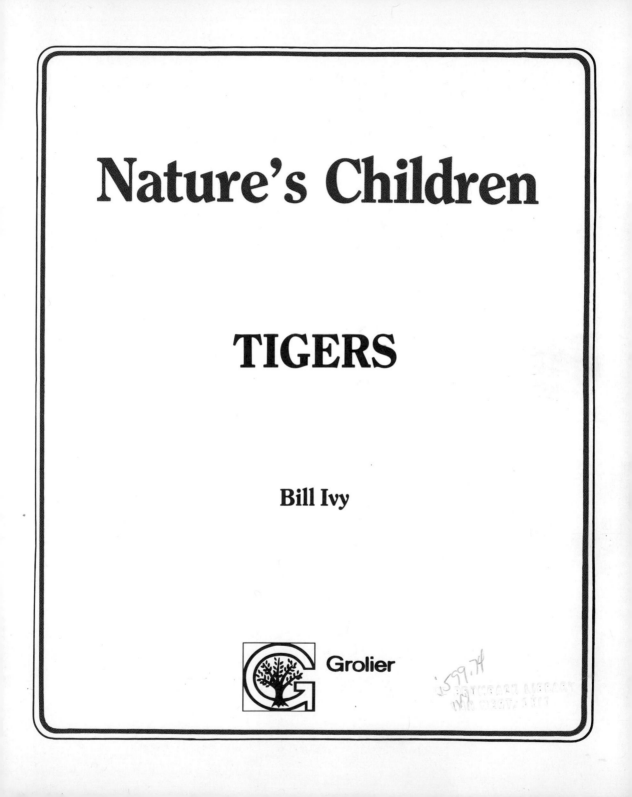

Grolier

FACTS IN BRIEF

Classification of the tiger

    Class: *Mammalia* (mammals)
    Order: *Carnivora* (carnivores)
    Family: *Felidae* (cat family)
    Genus: *Panthera*
    Species: *Panthera tigris*

Distribution. India, China, Indonesia.

Habitat. Varies widely. Tigers can survive almost any climate —hot or cold, dry or wet. Their only requirements are plenty of food and water and thick vegetation to provide cover when they hunt.

Distinctive physical characteristics. Reddish-orange to brownish-yellow fur, marked by black stripes and white patches; ruff of longer hair on some adult males; biggest member of the cat family.

Habits. Solitary; males mark territory with scent and by scratching; hunt mainly at night, usually searching out and stalking prey though they sometimes wait in ambush.

Published originally as
"Getting to Know . . . Nature's Children."

This series is approved and recommended by the Federation of Ontario Naturalists.

BB ER

This library reinforced edition is available exclusively from:

Grolier Educational Corporation
Sherman Turnpike, Danbury, Connecticut 06816

Contents

Fun and Games   Page 6

Tiger Territory   Page 9

Big Cats and Little Cats   Page 12

Tiger Types   Page 15

Tiger Eyes   Page 16

More Super Senses   Page 19

Heavyweights   Page 20

Quiet Feet   Page 23

Cool Cats   Page 24

Looking Good   Page 27

Meat Eaters   Page 28

An Undeserved Reputation   Page 31

On the Prowl   Page 32

No Trespassing   Page 35

Getting Together   Page 36

Cuddly Cubs   Page 39

Growing Up   Page 40

Lots to Learn   Page 43

Leaving Home   Page 44

Wild and Free   Page 46

Words to Know   Page 47

Index   Page 48

Everyone knows what a tiger looks like. Its bright orange coat and black stripes make it easy to identify.

Most of us will only ever see a tiger in a zoo, where its magnificent coat really stands out. Strange as it may seem, however, the bold pattern of the tiger's fur is not meant to attract admiring attention. On the contrary, it is actually designed to help the tiger blend in with its natural surroundings and stalk its prey unnoticed.

If you'd like to find out more about tigers and how they live, read on. You will surely agree with one of the most famous tigers that "they're grrrrreat!"

Fun and Games

Like most animal babies, tiger cubs love to play. They will probably snuggle up with mom for a nap after lunch, but before long they will be up and frisking about again. A good tussle or a game of peekaboo is always fun, and if the cubs get bored with that, there are butterflies to chase and bugs and beetles (not to mention each other's tails) to pounce at.

Meanwhile mom rests, seemingly unconcerned. You might even think she's asleep—but you'd be wrong. Just let one of the cubs move a step too far from her side and she will instantly call it back with a sharp grunt. The cub comes willingly. It will be a long time yet before these youngsters are ready to venture forth on their own.

A tiger mother raises her cubs alone.

Tiger Territory

You can find tigers living wild in parts of Russia, China, India and Indonesia. They are very hardy creatures, and can survive climates ranging from the hot, humid tropics to the cold, icy north. They may live in rain forests, dry woods, grasslands, swamps, marshes or snowy mountains. No matter where it makes its home, every tiger needs three things to survive: water, lots of food and enough thick vegetation to hide in while it stalks its prey.

Overleaf:
The Siberian tiger's thick coat helps keep it nice and warm, even in the snow.

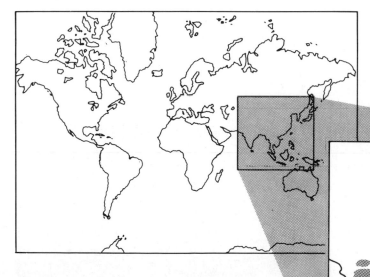

The colored areas on this map show where tigers live.

Big Cats and Little Cats

Tigers belong to the cat family, a family found all over the world. You may even have a member in your own home if you have a pet cat.

Zoologists divide all these cats into two groups: the big cats and the little cats. The little cats include house cats, lynx, bobcats, ocelots and cougars. Cougars? Don't those zoologists know how large cougars are? They do, but the distinction they make is between cats that roar and those that don't. Since cougars can't roar they don't qualify as biggies; tigers, lions, jaguars and leopards do.

And can you guess which one of these big cats is the biggest? Right—the tiger!

Now rare, the white tiger was once common in parts of India.

Tiger Types

There are several types of tigers and they differ in size and color depending on where they live.

The Siberian tiger of northern regions is the largest. It is yellowish in color and has an extra long, thick coat to protect it from the cold. It needs it! This tiger has to survive temperatures that drop as low as –45°C (–49°F). Brrr!

Tigers that live in the tropics, such as the Indian, South Chinese and Sumatran tigers, have shorter, thinner hair. These tigers also tend to be smaller and have more brightly colored fur.

A tiger's tongue is covered with short, sharp hooks that it uses to scrape every last bit of meat off a bone.

Tiger eye

Cat eye

Tiger Eyes

One of the first things you notice about a tiger are its piercing, yellow eyes. And those eyes are as sharp as they look!

A tiger's eyesight is much better than ours, especially in very dim light. Like a great many animals, however, tigers are colorblind and see everything in shades of black, white and gray. This means that they may have trouble spotting an animal that's not moving, no matter how close it is, because it often blends in with its surroundings. But as soon as the animal makes the slightest movement—watch out!

A tiger's eyes react differently to bright light than your pet cat's do. If you look at a cat's eyes when it is outside on a sunny day, you will see that its pupils are narrow, black slits. However a tiger's pupils close down to tiny circles.

A tiger does most of its hunting at night but may continue during the day if it has not been successful.

More Super Senses

What seems like an almost silent forest to us can be alive with sounds to a tiger. Its large, cup-shaped ears help focus sound and make the tiger very sensitive to even the slightest rustle. You can find out how this works by cupping your hands and holding them behind your ears. Notice how much louder everything sounds?

While less important to its survival than its hearing, the tiger's sense of smell is also well developed. In addition, around the tiger's face are long, coarse whiskers that it uses as feelers. Almost as handy as a spare set of eyes, these whiskers help the tiger maneuver around twigs and branches even in the blackest night.

The tiger's long canine teeth are as sharp as daggers.

Heavyweights

Tigers are definitely BIG cats. Males may be 3 metres (11 feet) long from the tip of their nose to the tip of their tail and weigh 170 kilograms (400 pounds). One super-heavyweight tipped the scales at 293 kilograms (645 pounds). Tigresses are smaller, usually not much more than 2.5 metres (a little over 8 feet) in length, and they weigh in at about 135 kilograms (300 pounds).

Is it just a coincidence that the biggest tiger, the Siberian, lives in the coldest area? No. A bigger body tends to lose heat more slowly than a smaller one. The Siberian's size helps it to survive its cold climate.

Given its size and strength, it is no wonder the tiger has few enemies.

Quiet Feet

Despite their size, tigers are very light-footed and can move silently through any terrain. The large, rubbery pads on the soles of their feet and the fur between their toes help muffle any noise. Tigers have five furry toes on each front foot, but the ''thumb'' toe is a little higher up the leg and does not touch the ground. Their back feet do not have this fifth toe. Like all cats, tigers walk on their toes and the balls of their feet.

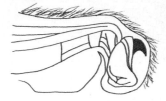

Claw retracted

Claw extended

Tigers' paws are equipped with sharp, curved claws that are perfect for hunting. When not in use the claws are drawn back into protective sheaths. This keeps them from being worn down as the tiger walks over hard ground or rocks. When needed, the claws can be extended in the wink of an eye. Most cats also use their claws for climbing, but tigers are too heavy to be good climbers and rarely leave the ground.

While playing, tigers are usually careful to keep their claws drawn in.

Cool Cats

All cats hate water, right? Wrong! Tigers love it and will often spend hours on a hot day just lying or standing in water to keep cool. They also find a quick dip very useful for cleaning insects and parasites out of their fur.

Because of their muscular shoulders and front legs, tigers are strong swimmers. Cubs learn to do the "cat paddle" while they are still quite young, and an adult can easily swim five kilometres or more (3–4 miles).

In the swim.

Looking Good

The tiger's striking reddish-orange or yellow fur is accented by jet black stripes and brilliant white markings. As well, many males have an attractive ruff of hair around their cheeks. Keeping such an elegant coat looking its best takes a lot of grooming, and the tiger spends a great deal of time each day licking itself clean.

Did you know that no two tigers look exactly alike? Each one has its own individual pattern of stripes that is as distinctive as your fingerprints. Even the markings on either side of a tiger's body do not match!

Even young tigers like to look their best.

Meat Eaters

Tigers eat meat and lots of it. They have enormous appetites and can eat up to 25 kilograms (55 pounds) at one meal. They average a good deal less than that over several days, however, and they often go for a week or more without eating anything.

Tigers prey mainly on deer, antelope and wild pigs, but they will eat almost anything that they can catch. This may be as small as frogs, turtles, fish and birds, or as large as water buffalo, elk, rhinoceros and elephant calves. When wild prey is scarce they may turn to an easy-to-catch meal of domestic cattle or goat.

Sometimes tigers swallow a few mouthfuls of grass and soil, probably to help in digestion.

Notice how the coat of this Bengal tiger helps it blend in with its surroundings.

An Undeserved Reputation

Tigers are shy and secretive, and they usually stay well away from human beings. Most will, in fact, run away if they catch sight of one. How then did tigers acquire their fearsome reputation as maneaters?

Tigers have been known to attack people on occasion. Usually it will be a mother protecting her cubs from someone who is getting too near her den. And sometimes it may be a tiger that is old or crippled or unable for some other reason to catch its normal prey. It may, for instance, have painful porcupine quills in its mouth, which not only make it irritable but make hunting game almost impossible.

Tigers are certainly dangerous, but they are not the deliberate maneaters that exaggerated stories would have you believe.

A tiger will normally drink several times during a meal.

On the Prowl

The black and orange hunter slinks silently through the forest. It carefully places each paw so that no sound will give it away. Pausing from time to time, it watches and listens. Then it continues its stalk.

Instead of searching out its prey, a tiger may try to ambush it—especially at water holes, where many animals gather. Whenever possible it will seek out an old, sick or lame animal that is not very fast. This big cat can only run quickly for about 25 metres (80 feet), so it must creep in very close before it attacks. Hunting at night helps it approach undetected.

Tigers are good hunters, but usually their prey is quick and gets away safely. The tiger knows there is no point in giving chase and simply moans quietly as it walks away frustrated. But when it is successful, probably only once in 15 or 20 tries, it lets out a victorious roar than can be heard a long way away!

Crouched and ready to pounce!

No Trespassing

Every tiger has its own territory where it lives and hunts. A male may share his domain with one or more females, but other males are not welcome and any bold enough to trespass are inviting trouble.

A tiger's territory may be about 65 square kilometres (25 square miles) if there is lots of food, or up to ten times that size if food is scarce. Obviously it is impossible for a tiger to guard all this land, so instead it regularly patrols its area and posts ''no trespassing'' signs. How? It scratches trees with its claws and scrapes the ground with its hind feet. And every so often it sprays the trees, rocks and bushes with its strong-smelling urine. These scrapes and scent markers let other tigers know that this property is spoken for. They may also allow male and female tigers to follow each other during the mating season.

On the prowl.

Getting Together

Tigers are loners and spend most of their lives by themselves. But if two tigers should meet, they will greet each other the way most cats do by touching cheeks or rubbing the sides of their bodies together. Once these formalities are over the two tigers go their separate ways.

The only time tigers come together is occasionally to share a meal or to mate. A male may follow a female's scent markings to locate her, or the two will roar back and forth until they find each other. If two males are interested in the same tigress they may fight, sometimes very fiercely. The female is not always impressed by these battles, however, and may end up choosing the loser or walking away from both of them!

Getting acquainted.

Cuddly Cubs

When the time comes for the mother tiger to give birth, she selects a suitable nursery. Tigers usually have a number of dens scattered throughout their territory, and the tigress will choose one that is well sheltered and close to water. She gives birth to anywhere from one to six babies, although the usual number is two or three. The cubs are about the size of small house cats and weigh around 1 kilogram (2 pounds). They are blind, helpless and totally dependent on their mother for care and protection.

Newborn tiger cubs spend most of their time drinking their mother's milk and sleeping. Their fluffy coats already show a striped pattern, and their feet seem much too large for their little bodies. It will be about two weeks before their eyes open and they get their first look at the world.

Growing Up

Tiger cubs grow very quickly. By the time they are six weeks old they may already weigh five times as much as they did at birth. Like all kittens, the cubs wrestle, tumble, stalk and snarl at each other. Sometimes the play can get quite rough, but it is just for fun and no one gets hurt.

By now these frisky youngsters are ready to leave their den for brief periods, and soon they will be venturing farther afield, tagging along close behind their mother. They keep track of her in the tall vegetation by following the white spots on the back of her ears. Should they lose sight of her they meow loudly.

When the cubs are about six months old they are ready to eat meat. While their mother is out hunting they stay hidden away in the den. But as soon as she returns they come bounding out to eat their dinner. The tigress waits to eat until all her cubs have finished.

If a tigress has to move her cubs before they are able to follow her, she will carry them one at a time by the scruff of the neck.

Lots to Learn

Before the young tigers can survive on their own, they have many important lessons to learn. First and foremost is the art of hunting.

The cubs were already preparing for this when they were playing and tumbling with their brothers and sisters. Now they watch their mother in action and begin sharpening their own skills by chasing after small game.

Becoming skillful hunters is difficult, and cubs may be hurt or even killed by their prey. It takes a lot of time and practice, and it will be well over a year and a half before the young tigers can effectively make their own kills. Their mother is very patient and helps them all she can.

Tigers in the wild may live to be fifteen years old.

Leaving Home

By one year of age the male cubs are almost as large as their mother and the females are just a little smaller. In another year or so they will be ready to leave their mother to make room for her next litter. Although adult tigers have few natural enemies, youngsters learning to get by on their own have to be wary of wild dogs, which may attack in packs.

Sometimes brothers and sisters remain together for a while before splitting up to find hunting grounds of their own. When they are three years old they are ready to seek out mates and start their own families.

Wild and Free

The human population of the world has grown enormously in this century, causing a serious problem for tigers. As more and more of their habitat has been turned into farmland, they have been pushed into ever smaller areas that can support them only in dwindling numbers.

Fortunately, things are beginning to look up for tigers. Countries where they live have passed laws to protect them and created reserves where they can live and hunt undisturbed. Maybe someday you will be lucky enough to visit one and see these beautiful animals prowling wild and free.

Until then, use your imagination. Picture a meadow at the edge of a dense forest. The last light of day is fading. Suddenly, unannounced by any sound, a tiger looms above the tall grass. Slowly, silently, its eyes shining in the semi-darkness, the huge cat advances . . . then stops. What is it? A sound? An odor? Something—for with a flick of its striped tail, the magnificent creature blends into the trees and swiftly, mysteriously disappears.

Words to Know

Cub   Name for the young of various animals including the tiger.

Den   Animal home.

Groom   Brush or clean hair or fur.

Habitat   The area or type of area in which an animal or plant naturally lives.

Litter   Young animals born at the same time.

Mate   To come together to produce young.

Parasite   An animal or plant that grows and feeds on or in another one.

Pupil   The opening in the center of the eye through which light enters.

Prey   Animal that other animals hunt for food.

Ruff   A collar-like growth of longer fur around the face of some animals, including some male tigers.

Territory   Area that an animal or group of animals lives in and often defends from other animals of the same kind.

Tigress   Female tiger.

Zoologist   Scientist who studies animals.

INDEX

babies. *See* cubs

claws, 23, 35
climbing, 23
coat, 5, 15, 27
cubs, 6, 39, 40, 43, 44

den, 39
description, 5, 9, 19
diet, 28, 40
distribution, 9
  map, 9

ears, 19
enemies, 44
eyes, 16

family, 6
feet, 23
female, 6, 20, 35, 39, 40, 43

getting along, 6, 31, 36, 40, 44
growing up, 40, 43, 44

habitat, 9, 15, 46
hunting, 23, 28, 32, 43

lifespan, 43

locomotion, 23
male, 20, 35
mating, 35, 36

paws, 23
protection, 31, 35, 39

relatives, 12
roar, 12, 32

scent, 35
senses
  hearing, 19
  sight, 16
  smell, 19
  touch, 19
Siberian tiger, 15, 20
size, 12, 20, 44
strength, 31
stripes, 5, 27
survival, 9
swimming, 24

territory, 9, 35
types, 15

whiskers, 19

Cover Photo: Tony Stone Worldwide (Masterfile)

Photo Credits: Bill Ivy, pages 4, 17, 18, 21, 26, 33, 34, 45; Metro Toronto Zoo, pages 7, 10-11, 13, 14; Dennis DeMello (New York Zoological Society), page 8; Bill Meng (New York Zoological Society), page 22; ZEFA (Masterfile), page 25; Kamal Prasad (Valan Photos), page 29; Alan Wilkinson (Valan Photos), page 30; FPG International (Masterfile), page 37; Robert C. Simpson (Valan Photos), page 38; New York Zoological Society, page 41; Tony Stone Worldwide (Masterfile), page 42.